THE MODERN GUIDE TO
Sex Etiquette, Too!

Double Eagle
Press

THE MODERN GUIDE TO
Sex Etiquette, Too!

TOM CAREY

*Author of the best-selling
Modern Guide to Sexual Etiquette &
The Marriage Dictionary*

Copyright 1995 by Double Eagle Press. All rights reserved. No portion of this book may be used or reproduced in any manner whatsoever, without permission of the publisher, except in the case of reprints or reviews.

First published January 13, 1995.

Manufactured in the United States of America.

ISBN: 1-877590-90-8

Published by:
Double Eagle Press
1247 W. Wellington
Chicago, IL 60657

The Modern Guide To Sex Etiquette

TABLE OF CONTENTS

	WHEN WE LEFT OFF...	7
1.	**THE SEXUAL REVOLUTION:** *Turn, Turn, Turn Over Baby*	9
2.	**THE MATING RITUAL** *Still Dating After All These Years*	15
3.	**LOVE & MARRIAGE?** *Here Comes The Bride*	37
4.	**PARTS IS PARTS** *Tab A & Slot B*	55
5.	**HOLDING YOUR OWN** *Polite Solo Sex*	69
6.	**CONDOM ETIQUETTE** *Of Party Hats & Raincoats*	77
7.	**THE CLIMAX BLUES** *Coming & Going*	87
8.	**POLITE PREGNANCY** *Baby, Baby, Oh Baby!*	95

WHEN WE LEFT OFF...
Coitus Adviceus Interruptus

Little did I know, back in 1987 when I wrote *The Modern Guide To Sexual Etiquette*, how starved the world was for knowledge of sexual mores and manners. I realize now, a quarter of a million copies later, that we humans are still desperate for every scrap of sexual information we can get. No matter how arcane or bizarre. How else to explain the popularity of Oprah, Phil and all those other shows that entertain us day after day with the real life stories of all those chubby, big-haired folks from Trailer Park, Alabama?

Let's face facts. If the 80's was a difficult time for a human with a sex drive to know what to do with his or her private parts, then the 90's are downright wacky.

In the last few years I have received via the mail, sexual questions, problems, dilemmas, moral paradoxes and desperate pleas for help. And that's just from the U.S. Senate. I know that you, gentle reader, must too feel the desire to be better informed about what to do, what to say, and how to smell when grappling with the opposite sex. Why else would you, or your loved one, have plunked down $7.95 American for this?

So I give you *"The Modern Guide To Sex Etiquette, Too"*, a brand new collection of questions and answers, meant to provide a bit of relief to those whom the battle of the sexes has left wounded and hollering "medic!"

Herein lie the answers to all the difficult questions left unasked in Volume I. Answers to questions like "What, exactly, is a female condom?" and "What is a yeast infection and why do they have commercials about it during Monday Night Football?"

It's true that times have changed, and not necessarily for the better. But at its core, the problem of how to get somebody besides yourself interested in handling your genitals remain the same.

I hope this will help you.

The Sexual Revolution
TURN, TURN, TURN...OVER

"Everybody's doing it, doing it, doing it, everybody's doing it now."

Commander Cody

The Modern Guide To Sex Etiquette

Q. Is anybody having sex anymore?

A. It's difficult, I'm afraid, for those of us who grew up in the "Free-love" 60s, and the "If-it-feels-good-do-it" 70s to relate to those of you who came of age in the "Screw-your-neighbor" 80s and the "Got-a-recent-lab-report?" 90s.

After all, we got to do drugs, drink and have all the sex we wanted - completely guilt free! Well, the non-Catholics were guilt free, anyway.

We ate bacon and eggs and ham and eggs and steak and eggs. Who knew from cholesterol? "Lite" beers were for "lite"-weights. Jogging was something you did to your memory.

In the *Modern Guide To Sex* there is a chapter about the One Night Stand. Today, if you did such a thing, you'd have to have your head examined. Not to mention some other important body parts.

Lucky for my royalty statements, and for the human race, some things never change. No matter how dangerous or how silly sex looks, people still want to do it.

...Too

Q. Is the sexual revolution over?

A. There never really *was* a sexual revolution. What happened was, a large number of people hit their twenties at the same time in this country and, like twenty-year-olds throughout the history of the world, they spent every waking hour thinking about, talking about, writing songs about and having, sex.

Much to the annoyance of everybody else in the world, these self-absorbed American Baby Boomers affect everything and everyone.

Today, this "Pig-in-the-Python" population bulge is dealing with its collective mid-life crisis and is more interested in mutual fund investing and Newt Gingrich than it is in sex.

By the time these folks hit their "Golden Years" I'm sure Time Magazine will be running cover stories on retirement homes and the runaway demand for pacemakers and artificial hips.

Personally, I'm buying property in Sun City.

...Too

Q. Well then, what are we left with?

A. Well, as far as life, liberty and the pursuit of nookie goes, I would quote from that sergeant on Hill Street Blues who used to send the troops out with a "Hey! Let's be careful out there."

This is good advice, but I wonder if it goes far enough. Getting a condom, a blood test, and a private investigator's report before you nibble someone's privates is smart, but if you feel you need all that, will you *ever* know them well enough?

Besides the above, we're left with pre-nuptial agreements, earrings for men, nose rings for everyone, the Wonder Bra, breast implants, penile implants, phone sex lines, and the movie rating system.

Not to mention transvestites, transsexuals, Tipper Gore, Madonna, Jockey shorts with humorous puppets attached at the crotch, Oprah, Victoria's Secret, "gentlemen's" clubs, and Ann Landers as the country's foremost proponent of masturbation Plus, I think bell bottoms are coming back in style.

Be very afraid.

The Mating Ritual
STILL DATING AFTER ALL THESE YEARS

"Is she really goin' out with him?"

Joe Jackson

Q. Once and for all. What does it mean when a man says "I'll call you"?

A. Women need to think of this infamous little phrase as a man's version of the Hawaiian Islander's "Aloha."

It's an all-purpose word which can mean anything from "Hello", "Good-bye", and "Welcome", to "Have a Mai-Tai," among other things.

When a man says "I'll call you", what it mostly means is he won't. If he was *really* interested in you, wouldn't he be trying to worm his way into your apartment to grope you?

Context is important. The man who slows a bit as he drives by your place, gives you a shove out the door and hollers "I'll call you sometime," as he roars off and you tumble to the pavement, gravel flying, is telling you something different than the man who walks you to your door, squeezes your hand meaningfully and says "I'll call you every hour on the hour 'til we can be together again."

Of course, you're probably better off if neither of these men call you.

...Too

What "I'll Call You" Really Means

1. "I'll call you."

2. "I'll call you if my girlfriend goes out of town."

3. "I'll call you if my wife goes out of town."

4. "I'll call you if my drinking buddies go out of town."

5. "I'll call you when I know you're out so I only have to leave a message on your machine."

6. "I'll call you if I get desperate."

7. "I probably won't call you."

8. "I definitely won't call you."

9. "Maybe we'll run into each other around the neighborhood."

10. "Aloha."

...Too

Q. Sooner or later, most women I date ask where the relationship is "going?" Is this polite? Can't we just have fun?

A. Where in the world did you get the idea that dating is fun? Oh, I know you might be fooled into thinking that if you browse the personals ads in your Sunday paper, what with all those people who enjoy "dining, dancing, bowling and walking on the beach in the rain." But what dating is really about is nothing less than the genetically pre-coded propagation of the species.

You think you like your date's perfect hour-glass figure because it is aesthetically pleasing. In reality, the Neanderthal man inside you is checking her out as a curvy, buxom baby-making machine.

That's OK, etiquette-wise. It's the same for women. She's looking lovingly across the table at you, sure, but she's not thinking about how hot you are. She's wondering if she could have kids with someone who puts ketchup on everything, and if she did would the boys would get your receding hairline.

...Too

Q. I go out with lots of guys who are "just friends", even my old boyfriend. Is there anything wrong with that?

A. That depends. If *they* think it's a date and you're manipulating them into buying you dinner, flowers and tickets to "Phantom Of The Opera", then *you* deserve to have your credit ruined and to appear in a gossip column linked to Michael Jackson.

If everybody knows going into the deal that no romance is going to be involved *and* everybody pays their own way, then that's no problem.

Q. Why does it matter who pays?

A. I knew it! It matters because if a man pays, it's a date. He wants to change your mind about being "just friends." If he has no hope of doing this, you need to tell him up front, thereby avoiding an embarrassing scene in the restaurant when he reaches over to take your hand and gaze soulfully into your eyes just as you start playing footsy with the cute guy at the next table.

...Too

Q. How do I politely break up with someone?

A. The correct way for a man to break up with a woman is to begin acting as crummy and rotten as he can. Of course, being a man, he may have to go a couple of years before his gal notices, but after several thousand dollars in therapy she'll probably wise up and dump him.

There are a couple of ways to speed things up guys. Get her a nice, useful gift for Christmas, a cordless drill, say. Send her "Women Who Hate The Men Who Love The Women Who Hate Themselves" or one of those other relationship books.

If that doesn't work, just answer her truthfully the next time she asks you if her butt looks fat. That ought to do it.

If you're a woman, you should begin to go out a lot more often with your girlfriends. Tell your boyfriend that you and he both need some "space." Tell him you think it would be for the best if you both began to see other people. Make sure to say, "We can still be friends, can't we?"

...Too

Q. That's exactly what my girlfriend did to me! I thought everything was fine. What's the deal?

A. There's another guy. There's *always* another guy. Women never take a foot off first base without having one on second. Next time a woman starts hemming and hawing and crying and saying you're too good for her and it's all for the best, interrupt her and ask, "Who is he?"

The same can't be said for guys. Not that there *isn't* often another woman. There just doesn't *have* to be. Men will break up for lots of reasons. Sometimes all that "relationship maintenance" (y'know, talking and stuff) just seems like too darn much work. It could be that he finally got cable and he doesn't need to come over to catch ESPN2 at your place anymore. Or, he could have just forgotten that he even *has* a girlfriend. With two softball leagues a week, his regular tee time and the time he has to put in honing his GameBoy skills and all, it's hard for a man to keep all his obligations sorted out.

...Too

Q. Is there a correct way to have an office romance? Is it a good idea?

A. It wasn't until the Clarence Thomas hearings that I learned what a hotbed of lust and desire the workplace of the 90s is. I can only assume that a lot of you have inhaled too many Liquid Paper fumes for your own good.

Is anybody *working* out there? Or has hanging around the laser printer turned into the aging professional single's version of cruising Main Street?

I would say this about office romance, and for that matter, all romance. It's always wise to visualize what your life will be like after you get that one-way ticket to Dump City.

Picture, for example, your latest former flame at the moment he told you that he needed to find a woman whose hips were not as big as yours. What if you were co-workers? Imagine seeing that butt head's smiling face every morning in the coffee room.

Still think fooling around with the cute new guy in accounting is a good idea?

...Too

Q. So what's the correct way to meet someone?

A. I'll tell you, all this club joining and networking and want-ad placing just reeks a bit too strongly of desperation to me. Damn, people! Let's show a little restraint, shall we?

Joining a quilting circle or taking a fencing class or learning mime in order to meet "that special someone" is way lame. Besides, if you *do* meet someone at one of these contrived "young adult singles" activities they're going to be just as desperate and pathetic as you are. Ick!

Apparently, there are a lot of you with *too darn much time on your hands!* What to do? Write a novel, paint a picture, take a long walk, volunteer at some organization that helps people who have problems that are more serious than getting dates.

Do good stuff. And if you meet someone along the way, cool. If not, you'll still have the satisfaction of being a swell human being. And you won't end up with a lot of broken fencing foils and badly made quilts cluttering up your apartment.

Q. I just started seeing someone. I think there's potential for something long term. How often do I call her?

A. In the early stages of dating, you should keep your calls functional. When you call to ask her out, have a specific plan in mind. Don't just say "Wanna do somethin' Friday?" Say, "Wanna go to the Tractor-Pull Friday?" This shows that you have planned an evening, that you are taking care to entertain her and show her a good time and not just killing time until a woman with bigger hooters comes along.

Space out your calls. Women are, and rightfully so, a little more safety conscious than they used to be. If you seem too anxious, you'll scare her off. If you call her up several times a day to say "Just wanted to hear your beautiful voice," you'll scare her off. If you call her answering machine several times a day to leave affectionate little messages like, "Thinking of you and your sea-shell pink ears and your dainty little piggy toes", she'll probably call the cops. And if she doesn't, I will.

...Too

Q. How do I tactfully refuse a persistent suitor?

A. Lie. It's the only way. When someone puts their ego on the line and asks you out, you may respond in only one of two ways. You can say yes. Or you can say "I'd love to, but I can't because..." and fill in the blank with a believable excuse.

Carry a list of them with you when you go out for a night on the town. Be creative, but not too wild. There's nothing tackier than turning down a guy who wants to dance by saying you have recently had knee surgery and then hitting the floor at full mambo with the next one who asks because he's cuter and you saw him in the parking lot getting out of a Mercedes.

Q. Dating is such a dicey proposition these days. What do you think of these "pre-sexual relations contracts"?

A. I think we should shut down every law school in this country immediately.

...Too

10 Polite Excuses For Turning Down Geeky Guys

1. I have to wash my hair.

2. I have to wash my cat's hair.

3. I have to write a letter to my husband on death row.

4. I have to tweeze my mole.

5. I have to stay home and tape "Star Trek: Kirk Returns."

6. I have group accordion practice.

7. I have to polish my "Gone With The Wind" commemorative plates.

8. I have to water my Chia Pets.

9. I'm channeling the spirit of Elvis that evening.

10. I'll be out of the country on a top-secret spy mission.

Love & Marriage
HERE COMES THE BRIDE

"I knew the bride when she used to like to party, I knew the bride when she used to rock and roll"
Nick Lowe

Q. How can I tell if it's really love?

A. Women in love will feel like a character in an old Fred Astaire/Ginger Rogers movie. They'll tap dance around the office furniture singing Cole Porter tunes. They'll strike up conversations with strangers on the bus and say things like "Isn't it a beautiful day?" when it's 10 below and there's an ice storm.

Men in love will stop at the side of the highway and change a flat tire for a little old lady. They'll window shop at jewelry stores. Buying flowers for no particular reason will seem to them, for the first time, like a very good idea.

Men and women both will feel the uncontrollable urge to send cute 'n' cuddly greeting cards with sappy verses and cow-eyed cartoon characters gawking at each other. In short, they'll be a royal pain in the ass as far as everyone else in the world is concerned.

Being deeply and obviously in love is particularly unwise if you work in a place where sharp weapons are readily available. So, for your own safety, put a sock in it!

...Too

Q. I don't think I'm ready for marriage. Is it OK to just live together?

A. I used to think that living together was a good idea. Kind of a marriage dress rehearsal. You can see what your lover is really like in the morning, deal with the toothpaste tube and toilet seat issues *and* save a little rent money. However, while it may not *be* marriage in the wedding-ring-and-annoying-in-laws sense, it will *feel* like it, in the laying-around-the-house-in-sweat-pants-feeling-too-tired-for-sex sense.

The reason our culture has no handy title, like boyfriend or fiance or husband, for live-in lovers is that people are too polite to call you what you are - roommates who boff occasionally.

The problem with living together sans wedding vows is, you are putting your life "on hold." Why buy nice glassware, you figure, because when you get married you'll register for some. Which will probably lead to you serving drinks to important dinner guests in the jelly jars and souvenir beer mugs you've collected over the years.

...Too

Q. My best friend just got engaged to the biggest loser. I can't let her go through with it. What can I do?

A. Ah, yes. The age-old dilemma. Tell her what you really think of this guy and three things can happen. One, she comes to her senses, dumps the guy, hates you for being a self-righteous putz and never speaks to you again Two, she goes through with it, she lives happily ever after, hates you for being a self-righteous putz and never speaks to you again. Or, three, she goes through with it, they get divorced, she's miserable, she hates you for being a self-righteous putz and never speaks to you again. Are you beginning to notice a pattern here?

Do yourself a favor. Buy the goofy bridesmaid's dress, smile throughout the sham of a wedding, send a lovely gift and keep your yap shut. When she gets divorced a few years from now and asks you how she could have ever been so stupid, smile sweetly and say it could have happened to anybody.

...Too

Q. What if my fiancee lets herself go after we get married?

A. You've got to ask yourself, when you're thinking about marrying someone, not just "Do I really love her?", but "Will I still love her when she gains ten pounds, when she's cranky because of her little "monthly visitor", and when her mother decides unexpectedly to join us on our vacation to the Bahamas?"

"Will I still love her when she decides that I would feel better if I gave up beer? And cigars? And fried food? And golf? Will I still love her when she critiques my exquisite and unerring fashion sense by saying "You're not really going out dressed like that, are you?'"

If you can't honestly answer yes to all of these questions, it may be that you're the kind of guy who is better off staying single; free to spend the rest of your self-centered, pathetic little life in a studio apartment, watching stock car races on cable TV and eating Raviolio's straight out of the can.

...Too

Q. So there's no guarantee that she won't get fat, quit waxing her lip and stop wanting sex after we get married?

A. The first problem I see here is you wanting sex with a large woman with a mustache. Sheesh!

It's true, there are no guarantees about these things. On the other hand, she has no guarantee that you won't turn into a Cheetos-munching blob whose idea of a big night is sitting on the couch riding the remote back and forth between college hoops and soft porn.

However, if you are a devoted husband, and caring lover, you should expect a little nookie. And not the "OK-if-you-really-want-to-just-hurry-up" kind.

A man has every right to expect the woman who seemed sexually aroused by his every move before marriage to remain reasonably amorous after her vows. If it turns out that all her pre-nuptial passion was feigned, he'll be feeling, and rightfully so, that he bought himself a Jaguar that somehow turned into a Yugo the moment he drove it off the lot.

...Too

Q. But doesn't the passionate part of a relationship always slow down after marriage? Surely he can't expect me to be a sexual dynamo every night?

A. Why is that? A man has every right to expect a woman to be the same after their wedding as before.

Let's face it. You are hopeful that he loves you for your bright, sunny disposition, because you're warm and caring and kind. And he probably does. But he also loves your unquenchable sexual desire and that fact that you dress up in heels, swat him with a rolled up Tribune and call him "Sparky."

And you love him not only for his cute, crooked little smile and for the way he swallows his "L"s like Tom Brokaw does, but also for his drive, his ambition and his checkbook. How would you feel if he decided after the honeymoon that he was tired of the rat race and that your salary could support the two of you while he pursued his dream of building the world's largest collection of knitted Kleenex box covers?

...Too

Q. What do Kleenex box covers have to do with sex?

A. Good question. Uh, let's see. How do I say this? Attractiveness and sexuality in a woman is not necessarily analogous to attractiveness and sexuality in a man. What women find attractive and desirable in men is a combination of qualities that differs from woman to woman. Some women like a man who is laid back, some like intelligence, some ambition, some like a guy with a cool car and some like a man who can imitate all the goofy sounds the Three Stooges used to make. (Actually the latter is pretty rare.)

Looks mean less to women. It's a good thing, too, seeing as how almost all physically good-looking men are either gay or in a health club five hours a day working on their all-season artificial tan, doing endless sets of bicep curls and squat-thrusts, chatting with perky-bottomed, pony-tailed aerobics instructors and preening in front of the floor-to-ceiling mirrors gazing fondly at their rippling latissimus dorsi.

...Too

Q. So it's OK for a man to be a slob, but a woman has to diet and exercise and take diuretics so she can attain some arbitrary, Playboy centerfold, impossible-for-the-average-woman-to-acquire-without-plastic-surgery figure?

A. My, my, my. Somebody's cranky. Look, it's understandable that during courtship you show only your best side. Heck, you're trying to close a sale here. But little by little you *must* begin to be your real self before marriage. No matter how scary your real self might be.

It's not fair for a man who has been Sir Galahad-like in his behavior before marriage to begin farting in bed and trying to hold his new wife's head under the covers on the honeymoon. Nor should a woman who has aerobicized herself into to perfect wedding dress form and behaved like a sex-starved parolee from an all-girl chain-gang throughout her engagement announce at the wedding reception, "Thank God that's over with! No more oral sex! Now, gimme some cake!"

...Too

Q. How do I know for sure my marriage is over?

A. Like the man says, "If you have to ask, you already know." If you're thinking about the big D, and I don't mean Dallas, (don't you just love country music?) then there's probably a pretty good reason.

Men, if she still hasn't learned how to warm your chicken pot pie until the edges get brown and the goopy chicken stuff starts seeping out the sides the way you like it, call a lawyer. She's got something going on the side.

Ladies, if you discover a pair of lacy, perfumed underwear with "Cyndi" embroidered on them in the glove box of his car, that should tip you off that your marriage is in trouble. Or that he is leading a very interesting double life.

Q. So, after all is said and done, is there sex after marriage?

A. No, not really.

...Too

Parts Is Parts
TAB A & SLOT B

"My ding-a-ling, oh my ding-a-ling"

Chuck Berry

Q. Is penis size important?

A. Important for what? Prying open stuck windows? Whacking a burglar on the head? If you mean, is it important for sex, the answer is "sort of".

If your aim is to make someone pregnant the answer is pretty much the same as the one that Abe Lincoln gave when someone asked him how long he reckoned a man's legs ought to be. Supposedly, old Abe said "A man's legs ought to be just long enough to reach the ground."

Q. You mean my penis should be long enough to reach the ground?

A. Yeah, if you're doing push-ups. No, what I mean to say, Brainiac, is that it should be long enough to reach its destination, whatever that destination might be. Length doesn't have much to do with doing a reasonably competent job of sperm delivery.

Now, if you want to appear as a stud in porno films, you'll need to be more well endowed. And you'll

...Too

need some girth to go along with that length.

Porno star Long Dong Silver, an "actor" now immortalized in story, song and Senate subcommittee, had an oddly long, but skinny, unit. Poor old Long Dong had an abbreviated career due to his inability to "perform". See, it doesn't matter how big the rocket is if you can't get it to blast off.

Besides, most women say they are more interested in thickness and shape, as well as a kind of aesthetically pleasing quality, if that's an appropriate phrase. A woman's main source of sexual pleasure originates from the old clitoris and the surrounding area, (actually, it originates mostly in her brain, but I don't expect you to be able to deal with that yet) her insides don't really feel that much.

There *is* a Florida doctor who does an operation that's sort of like liposuction in reverse. He distributes body fat into the shaft of the penis thereby increasing its (I love this word) girth. I do not have his 800 number. Sorry men.

Q. All right, then, if you won't tell us how big a penis should be, at least tell us how big the average penis is.

A. Ah yes, the old American male need for stats. You know, it's guys like you who created the absurd market for baseball cards. You also probably play that stupid fantasy football league with other sports statistics geeks.

Men are forever ranking one another. Whether arm wrestling, matching paychecks, beating the over/under on the Hornets-Bulls game or checking the guy at the next urinal, men have a pathological need to know where they stand.

That's why they're forever after the women in their lives for information on their lovemaking ability. And their, well, ranking. It's not that a man wishes to become a better lover to satisfy his mate, or increase the pleasure and intimacy in his relationship, he just wants to move up in the standings. And he feels as passionate about this as he feels about his bowling average. Almost.

...Too

> OK, NOW, WHEN YOU SAY I'M THE BEST LOVER YOU'VE EVER HAD.... WHAT DO YOU MEAN EXACTLY WHEN YOU SAY THE "BEST"?

Q. Please! Just give us the numbers! And fantasy football is not stupid!

A. Hah, I knew it! OK, boys, get your pencils and scorecards (and rulers) ready.

In it's flaccid (that's soft, guys) state the average penis is from 3 to 4 and a half inches long. That changes with temperature and physical exertion.

When erect, the average penis is 5 to 7 inches long. Average erect circumference, which is more important to the ladies but less important in the locker room, is 1 and a half to 2 and a half inches. We'll wait a moment here while you run off in search of a Playboy and a ruler.

Q. Is it true what they say about Black men?

A. It's twue, it's twue. But not as twue as most white guys think. On average, blacks are about a quarter of an inch bigger than whites. Knowing this doesn't help much in the locker room, though, does it men?

...Too

A MAN'S MEASURING STICK...

```
| 1  2  3  4  5  6  7  8  9  10  11  12 |
|           one foot                    |
```

...shown actual size

Q. I can't relax and enjoy sex unless the lights are off. My husband insists that I'm beautiful and that he needs to see me. What can I do?

A. That's a problem? Most women who have been married for any length of time have to dress in a French maid outfit and dance around the room to Ravel's *Bolero* to get their husbands to look up from the TV just once. And even that only works during commercials.

Thanks to years of exposure to underfed fashion models and ads for breast enlargement creams, no American woman ever feels comfortable about her body. The good news is, men don't care. Men are able to compartmentalize body parts. They talk about breasts and legs and butts as though they were parts for a Chevy. If C. Everett Koop showed up on TV one day with a pair of 40DD breasts your husband would probably say, "whoa, check that rack."

So leave the lights on and let him enjoy the parts he enjoys. Maybe you'll learn to enjoy them, too.

...Too

Q. What do you think about breast implants?

A. As far as I'm concerned, if you think it'll make you (or someone you love) happy to have a couple of blobs of plastic sewn into your chest, why not?

Remember though, *you're* going to have to lug the things around for the rest of your life, *he* won't. No more jogging or sleeping on your stomach.

Boobs are swell (or should I say, swelled?) but they don't make much practical sense unless you're posing for the cover of *Cosmopolitan* or trying to inspire a budding popular novelist. Have you ever noticed that you can't read more than four pages of any novel today without finding a three paragraph description of the heroine's (pick one) proud, haughty, regal, firm, perky, pendulous, generous, conical, comforting, gravity-defying, supple, warm, tender, jiggling breasts? That spinning noise you hear is coming from Hemingway's grave.

As for your breasts, be reasonable. Limit your increase to a cup size or two. Going from a AA to a D can cause whiplash.

...Too

The Modern Guide To Sex Etiquette

10 Reasons To Get A Boob Job

1. I want to dress up as Dolly Parton this Halloween.

2. I want to have to visit the Foundations Department at long last.

3. I want to test the laws of gravity.

4. I want to pass the pencil test.

5. I want to make a few extra bucks by dancing at bachelor parties.

6. I love the feel of underwire.

7. I want to wear a strapless dress without having it fall down.

8. I want to stick dollar bills in my cleavage like they do in movies.

9. I want to have a place to rest my beer.

10. If I go braless, I want people to be able to tell.

...Too

Holding Your Own
POLITE SOLO SEX

"Looks like it's me and you again tonight, Rosie."
Jackson Browne

Q. I am a devout (religion deleted). The (member of the ministry of the religion deleted) told us in Sunday school that touching yourself is a sin and to remember that God is always watching us. Is that true?
A. Let's see, according to your minister God is a Peeping Tom. The theological implications of this are staggering. Picture Him sitting around in front of a wall of TV monitors with a few angels, zapping from channel to channel with the Holy Remote looking for horny kids. I can see Him now, with a bowl of popcorn yelling, "Hey, Gabriel, that Gardner boy is bopping his baloney again. Crank up the VCR!"

Sexual release is a healthy and normal part of life. (Although you wouldn't know it by listening to my married buddies on poker night, but I digress). When there is no one available to provide you with this release, it is considered perfectly proper to provide it for yourself. Just remember to lock the door first, and clean up after you're done.

...Too

Q. Isn't there a social stigma against men masturbating, but no such stigma against women?

A. Yeah, how 'bout that? *Cosmopolitan* can run an article about "Pleasuring Yourself: The New Sexual Frontier" along with a comparison chart on different brands of vibrators and still be displayed in supermarket check-out aisles next to the Butterfingers and the *Weekly World News*. I wonder how many copies *Esquire* would sell if it ran a cover story called "Jacking Off: Vaseline, Nivea or Elbow Grease?"

Or maybe *Playboy* should provide a bit more truth in packaging. How about this for a cover blurb: "Buy This Magazine and You Can Look At Pictures Of Naked 20-Year-Old Girls With Large Breasts While You Masturbate!" Then *Penthouse* could counter with "Yeah? Well We've Got Naked 20-Year-Old Girls, Too, And We Show Close-Ups Of Their Crotches." I tell ya, I'd love to see the day.

But back to your question. The difference between men and women when it comes to "Letting Your Fingers Do The Walking" is a lot like the differ-

ence between men and women in regular, two-person sex. Or in regular life, for that matter. Men are gross, hairy creatures, who look downright silly naked, even when not sporting a bulbous erection. A man holding up a Cindy Crawford poster with one hand is beyond silly.

Women, on the other hand, are silky smooth, good-smelling humans whose sexual plumbing is tucked up neatly inside them and who mostly enjoy solo sex in bubble baths or on bearskin rugs in front of fireplaces. (At least according to this copy of Penthouse that I'm holding up here with one hand).

Q. Shouldn't Pee Wee Herman be locked up for "doing it" in a dirty movie theater?

A. Oh, I don't know. Where would you rather have him do it? Carnegie Hall?

...Too

The Modern Guide To Sex Etiquette

VOCABULARY LIST
Names for the act of...well, you know.

Bopping The Baloney
Jerkin' The Gherkin
Slappin' The Salami
Polishing The Edsel
Jacking Up The Chrysler
Shaking Hands With My Best Friend
Wacking The Wiener
Spanking Frank
Wanking
Choking The Chicken
Whipping The Bishop
Having A Date With Rosie Palms
Boxing The Clown

And For The Ladies...
Riding The Electric Unicorn
(With Vibrator)

Ringing The Doorbell
Pushing The Man In The Boat Overboard

Condom Etiquette
OF PARTY HATS & RAINCOATS

"Of course I know what they're for. You fill them up with water and throw them off the roof!"
> *Hermie to the druggist in "Summer Of '42"*

Q. What is a female condom?

A. Let's face it ladies, all condoms, are female condoms. The fact is, women face the risk of pregnancy. Which means women must bear the responsibility of birth control. *Or* you could *trust* the men you make love with to care about you and your well being. (We'll pause here for a moment of rueful laughter).

There is a new product enthralling talk show hosts these days, a cone-shaped latex device, designed to fit inside a woman's vagina and to cover the outer portion of her genitals, too.

This, the manufacturers claim, will protect a woman from pregnancy and from sexually transmitted disease. Plus, it's big enough to huddle under in case of rain.

I'm afraid I have to stress here, ladies, that should you be afraid of catching a bunch of nasty diseases from your partner, you don't know him well enough to be having sex with him. Actually, you don't know him well enough to be in the same room with him.

Q. Who buys the condoms?

A. It used to be the sole responsibility of teenage boys to buy condoms. In an old American fertility ritual, a boy on the brink of manhood was sent alone into a drugstore. There he would stand for hours, looking at magazines, thumbing packs of baseball cards, sweating nervously and waiting for the female clerk to go on break so he could stroll, as casually as someone who has perspired two quarts can stroll, to the counter and say to the pharmacist, in a cracking voice, "Trojans please."

Once he bought them, the young man kept the "rubbers" in his wallet, removing them only for occasional fondling or to display them to awestruck pals.

Nowadays, four-year-olds know what condoms are for and may have actually bought some themselves. They are openly displayed at the supermarket, next to enemas, depilatories, suppositories and all the other personal stuff that we as a culture used to have the good sense to hide under a cloak of shame and secrecy.

Q. Should a woman offer to, uh, well...install the condom?

A. It's not *who* installs the condom that's important, it's *how*. It's perfectly acceptable for a woman to carry condoms, and perfectly acceptable for her to know how they work. Actually, it's imperative. If, however, when in the clinch with a new lover, she reaches under the bed and pulls out a large, colorful display of condoms in all sizes, styles and brands and begins waving them around like the Condom Fairy, she may be faced with the dilemma of how to wrap a rapidly deflating penis. Most men would like to believe that you haven't bedded thousands, safely or not.

Aside from using a little tact, then, go ahead. Remember, though, that an erection can be a delicate thing, so you ought to wait until you know him a little better before you say things like "Perhaps we should go to a smaller size, honey," or "Here, let's use this brand. It's ribbed, knobbed, lubed, studded and glow-in-the-dark!"

...Too

Q. Is it rude to carry condoms with you?

A. In the good old days, (I keep saying that, don't I?) if a man were to find himself happily engaged in a spontaneous act of passion and he were to suddenly produce a condom at the appropriate time, his lady friend might very well say, "Oh, so you planned to seduce me all along, eh? Do you think I'm just some easy piece of trash!?" And he might get a slap in the face.

It seems that folks used to believe that being prepared was just for boy scouts and that risk of pregnancy was all part of the thrill of sex. Which is probably why more teenaged girls got pregnant in 1958 than in 1988. (You can look it up).

Now, if you so much as offer to hold hands without proffering a note from your physician, a list of past sexual partners and practices *and* a condom you might get a slap.

The times they are a-changin'.

...Too

Q. When is the appropriate time to offer a condom?

A. The appropriate time is sometime after you first introduce yourself and before you are stretched naked across the bearskin rug in her living room with a rose in your teeth, oysters in your stomach, a song in your heart and an hour of foreplay in your immediate past. It's definitely before she says "You *do* have some protection, don't you, hon?"

Q. How do I bring up the subject?

A. You shouldn't have to. It'll bring itself up. Everywhere you look today there are images of sex and sexuality. From TV commercials to T-shirts, you can't escape it. If you want to be real subtle you could show her a photograph of a train going into a tunnel or the Washington Monument and say "Look, sweetie. Remind you of anything?"

...Too

The Climax Blues
COMING & GOING

"Hold on, baby, I'm coming"

Sam & Dave

Q. I can't climax during intercourse and my husband is very depressed about it. I never have any trouble when I use...well, other methods. Is there something wrong with me?

A. You mean besides the fact that you married an insensitive clod who would rather have you believe there's something wrong with you than try a little something besides the old missionary position? Hells bells, *most* women can't climax from intercourse alone! In one of God's amusing little pranks, he tucked the clitoris away in an area that is relatively unreachable via the old erection express. The onliest way to get ahold of that sucker is by hand. Or tongue. Or toe, or thumb or elbow for that matter.

If the Captain of Romance refuses to provide you with stimulation via one of the above, buy a vibrator, lock yourself in the bedroom with it and allow him to hear the results through the door. Perhaps he'll become inspired to learn some of those "other methods" himself.

...Too

Q. How can I tell if my wife really has an orgasm? Sometimes I think she's faking it.

A. Are you keeping score, or something? Why should she need to fake it? Have you let her know that her orgasm means more to you than it does to her? Is she afraid that your ego is so wrapped up in your sexual performance that she'd be afraid *not* to fake it?

The truth is, you probably can't tell. Physiologically speaking, there *are* a few sure signs of female orgasm. Many women get a warm blush across their chests. Most women's nipples become erect and extremely sensitive. At the moment of release her pelvic muscles will contract rapidly just like yours do, although you probably won't be able to verify this unless you insert a piece of scientific equipment in a very delicate place.

I doubt if you'll get her permission to do that, though, especially if you're so out of touch with her that you're still wondering about her faking it.

...Too

Q. Is faking it wrong?

A. Faking it can set a bad precedent. Do it on a regular basis and you'll have on your hands one of the most vexing characters in nature. A man who thinks he's a great lover who is actually a terrible lover. I hear a chorus of women now saying, "So? What else is new?" These women I cannot help.

What I will say, is this. If you don't feel up to a true roll in the hay, say it. Honesty is the best policy, in bed and in politics, although we rarely get either in this nutty world. Offer to give your man a "quicky". Tell him you're saving up for next time. Most men will be relieved that they don't have to worry about you and can just go ahead and please themselves. (An even larger and louder chorus of women saying "So? What else is new?")

It shouldn't take more than a couple of minutes of your time and then you'll be free to get back to your needlepoint or crossword puzzle.

Q. My husband always seems to be the initiator in our sexual relationship. Do men think it's OK for a woman to take control once in a while?

A. I conducted a scientific poll (OK, I talked to several guys I play softball with on the weekend and a couple of fellas sitting at the bar at my local pub) and turned up the following response.

I asked, "Would you enjoy it if the woman in your life dressed up in Victoria's Secret stockings and garter belt, undressed you slowly, gave you a hot oil massage and told you to just lay back and enjoy it while she climbed on and rode you like Secretariat?"

Four guys said "Yowza" or words to that effect, three guys said, "Hubba, hubba," and one guy gulped down his beer ran out the door saying he had urgent business at home to attend to.

I would interpret these responses to be an unqualified "Yup."

...Too

Polite Pregnancy
"OH, BABY!"

"She's having my baby, what a lovely way of saying how much ya love me."
Paul Anka

Q. I want to have kids and my biological clock is ticking! What can I do?

A. The late Jerry Rubin, former Yippie leader and investment banker, once said, "Never trust anyone over thirty." That was before he started wearing a suit and tie and selling junk bonds to retirees. Be that as it may, it was good advice for hippies in 1969. But it's bad advice for women in the 1990s who would like to have children before they go through menopause and have to have them surgically implanted.

The maturation time for young men in this country, never a rapid process in the best of times, has lengthened considerably in the last few decades. Your grandfather was probably working and married by the time he was 18. But that was during the Great Depression. (That's the historic Great Depression, not the time in college when you got dumped by your "true love" and spent Thanksgiving break in your dorm room eating cold turkey leftovers and cranberry sauce out of the can and watching a tape of "Gone With The Wind" over and over again).

...Too

These days, things are a bit different. Lots of men in their twenties are still "trying to find themselves" and "looking for their place in society". This has led to a profusion of bad haircuts, baggy shorts and backward baseball caps. Trust me, you could search every used CD store, alternative book store and hip coffeehouse in the world, line up every clove cigarette smoking male you can find discussing the artistry of Eddie Vedder and the pros and cons of nipple rings, and you'll not find decent husband material in the bunch.

Q. So, like, what is their problem?

A. Anthropologically speaking, men are like many of the prehistoric dinosaurs. If you remember sixth grade science, you'll recall that some dinosaurs had a small brain in their head and another, auxiliary brain, in their tail. Men are built much the same way, only they don't have a tail, if you get my drift.

Younger men are governed primarily by this sec-

...Too

ond brain and they'll follow it wherever it may lead - to late night bars, strip clubs, adult video stores, your sister's underwear drawer, the foundations department at Sears, etc.

As a man ages, brain #1 begins to affect his behavior more and brain #2 less. This trend continues until he reaches middle-age, when a man can often can recall golf courses he once played in startling detail but totally forget what his penis is for.

You need to look for a man about 30 years-old. At this age his nether brain is still in enough control that he'll be entranced by your perky little bottom, but he also will have begun to show an interest in marriage, kids, a job and apartment furnishings that didn't used to contain beer or pizza.

Date a younger man and you're fooling with an over-grown teenager, date an older one and you'll have a man more interested in his golf game than sex. At least until he has his mid-life crisis. Or gets elected to public office.

...Too

Q. My wife is pregnant with our first. When do we have to stop having sex?

A. Immediately! You want to have sex with the mother of your own child?! That's sick!

Q. What? Gee, I never thought of tha...hey! Wait a minute!

A. All right, all right. If you insist. Although I'd like to remind both of you that sex is what got you into this fix in the first place. There's nothing wrong with doing what comes naturally at any point during pregnancy, as long as there is no discomfort or danger to your wife or child. If she feels like it, and God knows how she could, what with vomiting, backaches, hemorrhoids, varicose veins, diminished bladder control and all. But if she does feel like it, it's generally OK. Check with your doctor, first.

Q. How soon can we start making love again after she gives birth?

A. As your friends and relatives who are already parents will no doubt tell you, this is pretty much a moot question.

Just ask them about poopy diapers, 3AM feedings, sore, leaky nipples, sleep deprivation, spitting up, stretch marks, episiotomies, sitz baths and mothers-in-law who move in to the guest room "to help out for awhile" and end up staying for three months.

Then reread chapter 5, *"Holding Your Own."*

...Too

About the Author:
Tom Carey is the author and illustrator
of several books, including:
The Marriage Dictionary,
The Club Thrower's Handbook and
Teed Off! The Modern Guide To Golf.

He is married and lives in Chicago,
where he dispenses free advice and
sage wisdom to all his friends and
relatives who listen to him
not one little bit.

Also available from
Double Eagle Press:

The Marriage Dictionary	$ 6.95
The I Love To Fart Diet	$ 6.95
The Modern Guide To Sex, Too!	$ 7.95
Teed Off! A Modern Guide To Golf	$ 7.95
The Club Thrower's Handbook	$ 9.95
Your Baby: An Owner's Manual	$ 7.95
Baby's 40th Birthday Book	$10.95

Double Eagle Press
books are distributed through
**Sourcebooks, Inc.
1-800-SBS-8866**